Popular Performer

1940s and 1950s Love Songs

Arranged by CAROL TORNQUIST

The Best Romantic Classics

The 1940s and 1950s have a stunning array of memorable and m___ ___ ___ songs. This collection revisits these great hits, casting them in the rich voice of the piano. Popular songs that have become jazz standards are represented, such as "Angel Eyes" (1946), "Taking a Chance on Love" (1940), and "You Stepped Out of a Dream" (1940), as well as songs that won prestigious awards. Academy Award winners for Best Original Song include: "Love Is a Many-Splendored Thing" (*Love Is a Many-Splendored Thing*, 1955), "Secret Love" (*Calamity Jane*, 1953), and "Three Coins in a Fountain" (*Three Coins in a Fountain*, 1954). "Volare," as sung by Domenico Modugno, won the Best Song of the Year and Best Record of the Year at the very first Grammy Awards ceremony in 1958. "Misty" was inducted into the Grammy Hall of Fame twice—in 1991 for the original recording by jazz pianist Erroll Garner and in 2001 for the recording by Johnny Mathis. The whimsical rhythms of "Catch a Falling Star," the powerful climax in "I Wanna Be Around," and all of the other wonderful musical moments are certain to provide hours of enjoyment for the pianist who wishes to be a *Popular Performer*.

CONTENTS

ANGEL EYES

Words by Earl Brent
Music by Matt Dennis
Arr. Carol Tornquist

At Last

Music by Harry Warren
Lyrics by Mack Gordon
Arr. Carol Tornquist

CATCH A FALLING STAR

Words and Music by
Paul Vance and Lee Pockriss
Arr. Carol Tornquist

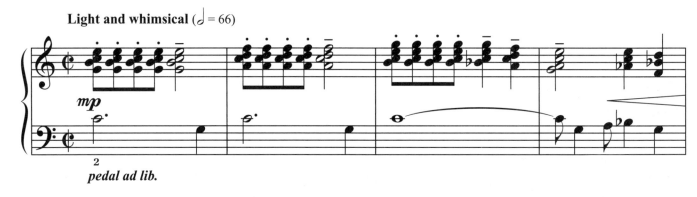

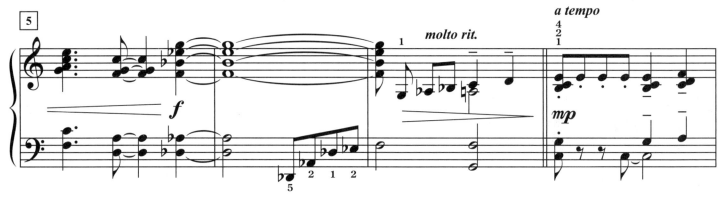

A Certain Smile

Music by Sammy Fain and Paul Francis Webster
Arr. Carol Tornquist

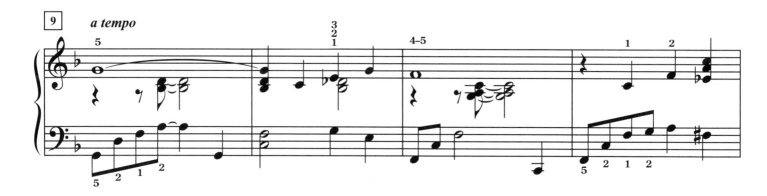

I Wanna Be Around

Words and Music by
Johnny Mercer and Sadie Vimmerstedt
Arr. Carol Tornquist

Love Is a Many-Splendored Thing

Music by Sammy Fain
Lyrics by Paul Francis Webster
Arr. Carol Tornquist

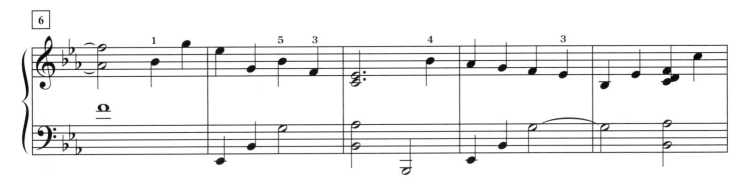

MISTY

Music by Erroll Garner
Arr. Carol Tornquist

Secret Love

Words by Paul Francis Webster
Music by Sammy Fain
Arr. Carol Tornquist

Simply and with expression (♩ = 112)

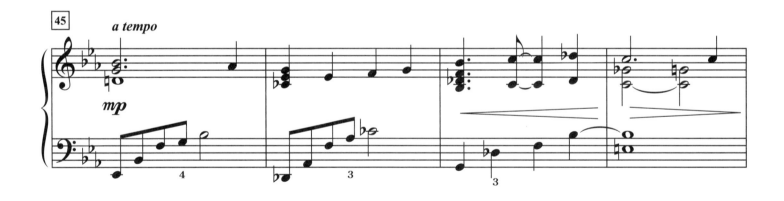

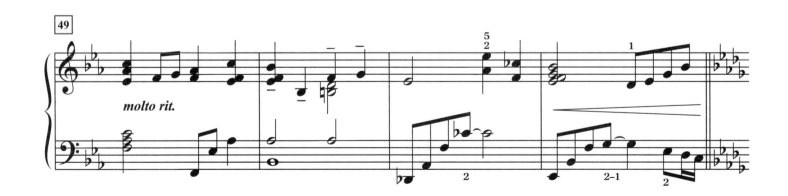

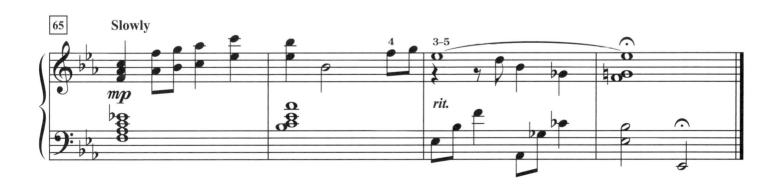

Taking a Chance on Love

Music by Vernon Duke
Words by John Latouche and Ted Fetter
Arr. Carol Tornquist

Three Coins in a Fountain

Music by Jule Styne
Words by Sammy Cahn
Arr. Carol Tornquist

You Stepped Out of a Dream

Music by Nacio Herb Brown
Lyrics by Gus Kahn
Arr. Carol Tornquist

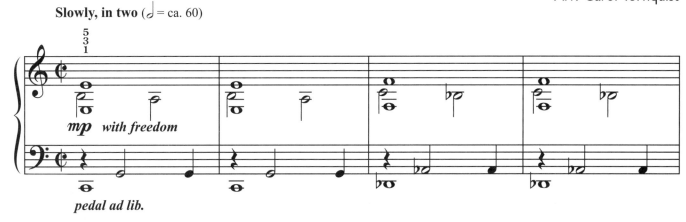

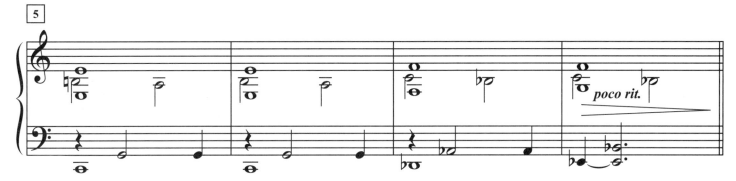

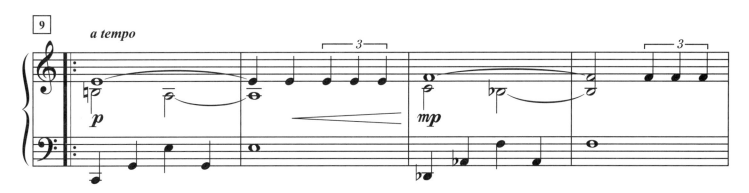

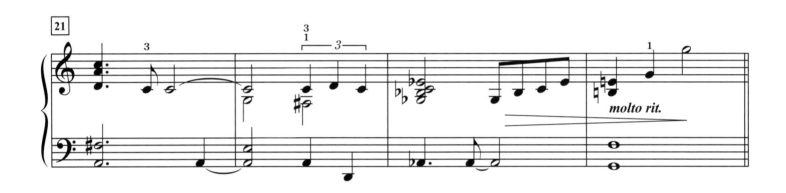

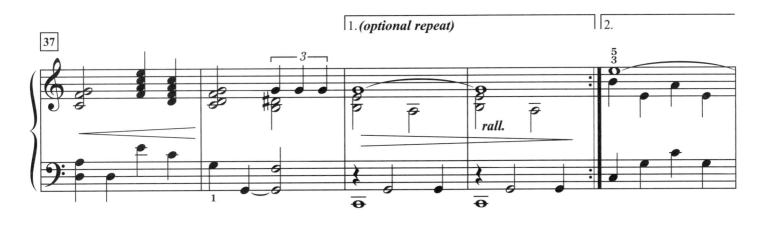

VOLARE

Music by Domenico Modugno
Arr. Carol Tornquist

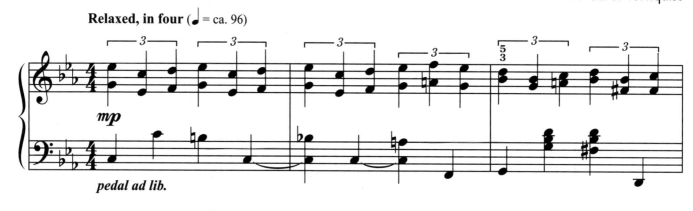